From Accident to Hospital

Anastasia Suen

rourkeeducationalmedia.com

*Scan for Related Titles
and Teacher Resources*

Teaching Focus:

Phonics: Word Study- Count the syllables in the words paramedic and doctor. Which word has more syllables? Which word has more letters?

Before Reading:

Building Academic Vocabulary and Background Knowledge

Before reading a book, it is important to set the stage for your child or students by using pre-reading strategies. This will help them develop their vocabulary, increase their reading comprehension, and make connections across the curriculum.

1. *Read the title and look at the cover. Let's make predictions about what this book will be about.*
2. *Take a picture walk by talking about the pictures/photographs in the book. Implant the vocabulary as you take the picture walk. Be sure to talk about the text features such as headings, Table of Contents, glossary, bolded words, captions, charts/ diagrams, or Index.*
3. Have students read the first page of text with you then have students read the remaining text.
4. *Strategy Talk – use to assist students while reading.*
   - *Get your mouth ready*
   - *Look at the picture*
   - *Think…does it make sense*
   - *Think…does it look right*
   - *Think…does it sound right*
   - *Chunk it – by looking for a part you know*
5. *Read it again.*
6. *After reading the book complete the activities below.*

Content Area Vocabulary
Use glossary words in a sentence.

911
ambulance
Emergency Room
EMT
paramedic
stretcher

After Reading:

Comprehension and Extension Activity

After reading the book, work on the following questions with your child or students in order to check their level of reading comprehension and content mastery.

1. *Why is it important for cars to pull over when they see an ambulance with its sirens on? (Inferring)*
2. *Why is the word ambulance spelled backwards on the hood of the vehicle? (Summarize)*
3. *Have you ever met an EMT, firefighter, or 911 operator? Tell us about it. (Text to self connection)*
4. *Which jobs in the book work together? How do they work together? (Asking questions)*

Extension Activity

Draw it out! After reading the book, draw out the events that happened. You should create a picture from the car accident to the hospital. After you have completed drawing your picture, retell the story to a parent, teacher, sibling, or classmate.

Oh, no! There has been an accident!

Someone calls **911**.

A 911 operator answers the call.

Job Shop

There are 911 operators at work day and night.

The 911 operator calls for the police and an **ambulance**.

6

The ambulance at fire station 51 gets the call.

Job Shop

Some people call an ambulance a bus or a truck.

Two people work together in an ambulance. They are the **paramedic** and the **EMT**. The EMT is the ambulance driver.

Job Shop

Ambulance workers are trained to give first aid in an emergency.

Job Shop
EMT stands for Emergency
Medical Technician.

The EMT drives the ambulance with sirens and lights on. The cars and trucks on the road pull over to the side.

Wooo Wooo Wooo

Job Shop

It's the law. You must move out of the way when an ambulance comes.

The ambulance arrives at the accident.

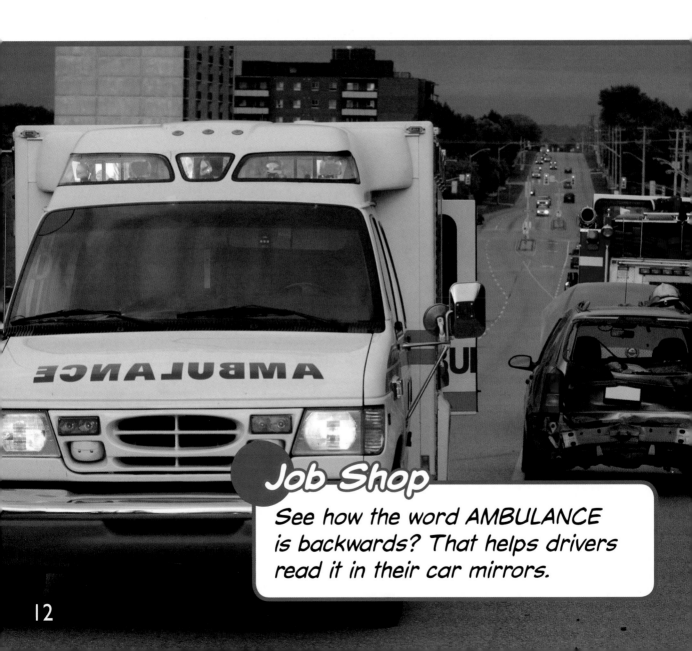

Job Shop

See how the word AMBULANCE is backwards? That helps drivers read it in their car mirrors.

The police officer is already there directing traffic away from the accident.

The EMT and paramedic put the patient on a **stretcher**. The paramedic treats the patient. The EMT helps.

Job Shop

The person hurt in an accident is called the patient.

The paramedic rides in the back of the ambulance with the patient.

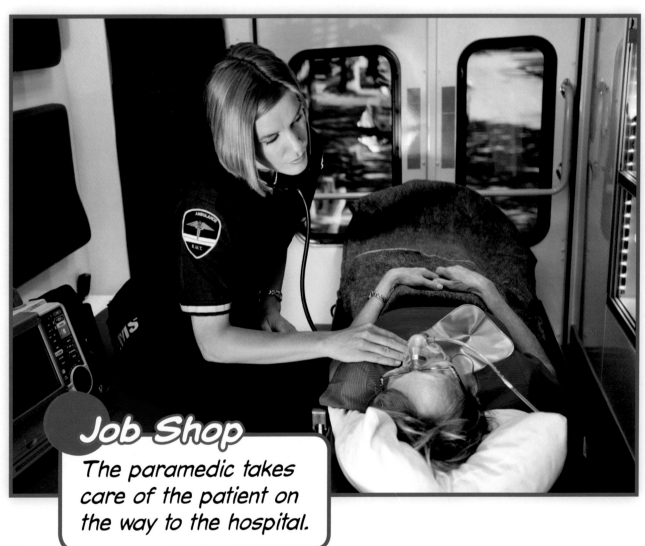

Job Shop
The paramedic takes care of the patient on the way to the hospital.

The EMT drives the ambulance to a hospital's **Emergency Room**.

Job Shop
Part of the job of being an EMT is knowing the way to every hospital in the city.

The paramedic tells the nurse and the doctor about the patient.

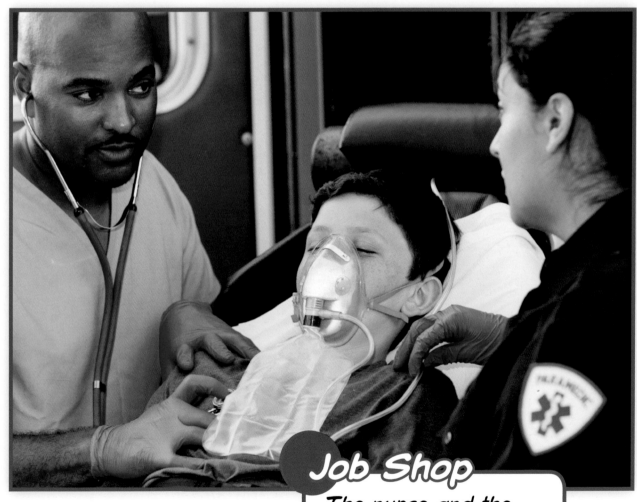

Job Shop
The nurse and the doctor take over now.

The doctors and nurses take the patient to a hospital room.

Job Shop

The nurse and the doctor check the patient. The doctor decides what to do next.

The doctor wants to see inside the patient's leg. A technician will take an X-ray.

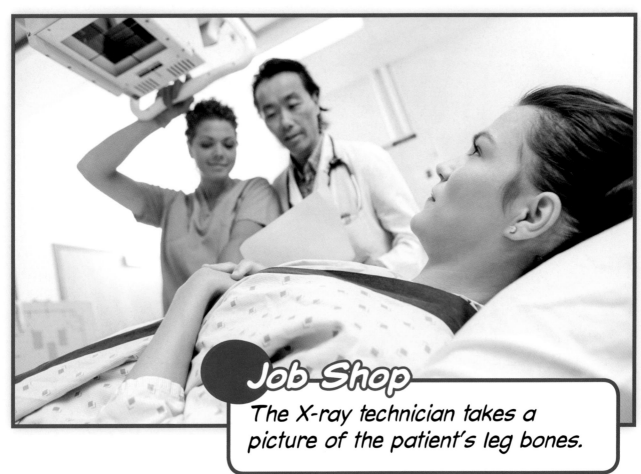

Job Shop

The X-ray technician takes a picture of the patient's leg bones.

The patient's leg is broken. The doctor puts a cast on the patient's leg so it can heal.

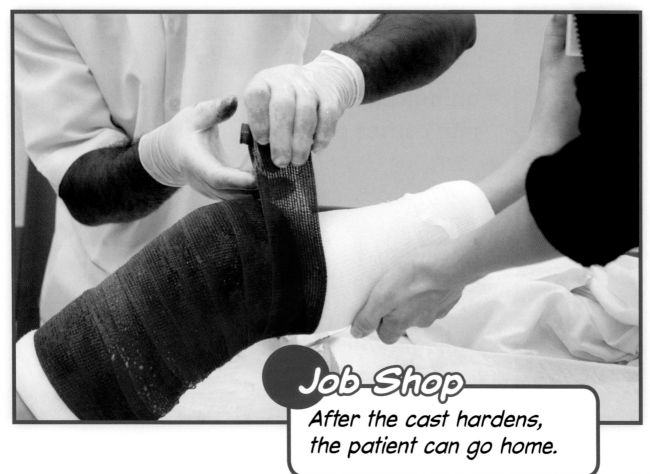

Job Shop

After the cast hardens, the patient can go home.

Photo Glossary

 **911** (NINE-ONE-ONE): The phone number to call for help with an emergency.

 **ambulance** (AM-byuh-luhns): A truck that carries people to the hospital.

 **Emergency Room** (ih-MUR-juhn-see ROOM): The part of the hospital for patients with emergencies.

 **EMT** (EMT): The person who drives the ambulance and helps the paramedic.

 **paramedic** (par-uh-MED-ik): A person trained to do emergency first aid.

 **stretcher** (STRETCH-er): A bed with handles and wheels.

Index

Websites to Visit

www.911forkids.com/

www.911.gov/whencall.html

kidshealth.org/kid/watch/er/911.html

About the Author

Anastasia Suen rode inside an ambulance after a car accident when she was ten years old. Her broken leg took all summer to heal. The author of 190 books for children, she lives with her family in Plano, Texas.

Meet The Author!
www.meetREMauthors.com

© 2015 Rourke Educational Media

www.rourkeeducationalmedia.com

PHOTO CREDITS: Cover © Jelena Popic, Monkey Business Images; title page © January Jones; page 3, 4, 9 © Monkey Business Images; page 5 © FEMA/ Mark Wolfe; page 6 © Lisa F. Young; page 7 © OgnjenO; page 11 © Glen Jones; page 12 © Dan Bailey, page 13 © Harry Hu/Shutterstock; page 15 © Michaeljung; page 16, 19 © Tyler Olson; page 17 © bgpix; page 18 © kali9; page 20 © Leaf; page 21 © Richard J Gerstner

Edited by: Luana Mitten

Cover and Interior design by: Jen Thomas

Library of Congress PCN Data

From Accident to Hospital / Anastasia Suen

(Little World Communities and Commerce)

ISBN (hard cover)(alk. paper) 978-1-63430-058-2

ISBN (soft cover) 978-1-63430-088-9

ISBN (e-Book) 978-1-63430-115-2

Library of Congress Control Number: 2014953335

Printed in the United States of America, North Mankato, Minnesota

Also Available as:

SUPERMAN
REBIRTH DELUXE EDITION
BOOK 2

SUPERMAN
REBIRTH DELUXE EDITION
BOOK 2

PETER J. TOMASI and PATRICK GLEASON * MICHAEL MORECI
writers

PATRICK GLEASON * DOUG MAHNKE * JORGE JIMENEZ * IVAN REIS * JOE PRADO
RYAN SOOK * ED BENES * CLAY MANN * TONY S. DANIEL * SEBASTIÁN FIUMARA
SCOTT GODLEWSKI * MICK GRAY * SANDU FLOREA * SETH MANN * JAIME MENDOZA
RAY McCARTHY * JOE PRADO * KEITH CHAMPAGNE * SCOTT HANNA * MATT SANTORELLI
artists

JOHN KALISZ * ALEJANDRO SANCHEZ * MARCELO MAIOLO * RYAN SOOK
DINEI RIBEIRO * ULISES ARREOLA * DAVE STEWART * WIL QUINTANA * HI-FI
colorists

ROB LEIGH * SAIDA TEMOFONTE * DAVE SHARPE
letterers

PATRICK GLEASON and JOHN KALISZ
collection cover artists

JORGE JIMENEZ and ALEJANDRO SANCHEZ * PATRICK GLEASON, MICK GRAY and
JOHN KALISZ * RYAN SOOK * IVAN REIS, OCLAIR ALBERT and MARCELO MAIOLO
SEBASTIÁN FIUMARA and DAVE STEWART * PATRICK GLEASON and JOHN KALISZ
LEE WEEKS and BRAD ANDERSON
original series covers

SUPERMAN created by **JERRY SIEGEL** and **JOE SHUSTER**
SUPERBOY created by **JERRY SIEGEL**
By special arrangement with the Jerry Siegel family

EDDIE BERGANZA Editor – Original Series * **ANDREW MARINO** Assistant Editor – Original Series * **JEB WOODARD** Group Editor – Collected Editions
SCOTT NYBAKKEN Editor – Collected Edition * **STEVE COOK** Design Director – Books * **LOUIS PRANDI** Publication Design

BOB HARRAS Senior VP – Editor-in-Chief, DC Comics * **PAT McCALLUM** Executive Editor, DC Comics

DIANE NELSON President * **DAN DiDIO** Publisher * **JIM LEE** Publisher * **GEOFF JOHNS** President & Chief Creative Officer
AMIT DESAI Executive VP – Business & Marketing Strategy, Direct to Consumer & Global Franchise Management
SAM ADES Senior VP & General Manager, Digital Services * **BOBBIE CHASE** VP & Executive Editor, Young Reader & Talent Development
MARK CHIARELLO Senior VP – Art, Design & Collected Editions * **JOHN CUNNINGHAM** Senior VP – Sales & Trade Marketing
ANNE DePIES Senior VP – Business Strategy, Finance & Administration * **DON FALLETTI** VP – Manufacturing Operations
LAWRENCE GANEM VP – Editorial Administration & Talent Relations * **ALISON GILL** Senior VP – Manufacturing & Operations
HANK KANALZ Senior VP – Editorial Strategy & Administration * **JAY KOGAN** VP – Legal Affairs * **JACK MAHAN** VP – Business Affairs
NICK J. NAPOLITANO VP – Manufacturing Administration * **EDDIE SCANNELL** VP – Consumer Marketing
COURTNEY SIMMONS Senior VP – Publicity & Communications * **JIM (SKI) SOKOLOWSKI** VP – Comic Book Specialty Sales & Trade Marketing
NANCY SPEARS VP – Mass, Book, Digital Sales & Trade Marketing * **MICHELE R. WELLS** VP – Content Strategy

SUPERMAN: REBIRTH DELUXE EDITION BOOK 2

Published by DC Comics. Compilation and all new material Copyright © 2018 DC Comics. All Rights Reserved.

Originally published in single magazine form in SUPERMAN ANNUAL 1 and SUPERMAN 14-26. Copyright © 2016, 2017 DC Comics. All Rights Reserved. All characters, their distinctive likenesses and related elements featured in this publication are trademarks of DC Comics. The stories, characters and incidents featured in this publication are entirely fictional. DC Comics does not read or accept unsolicited ideas, stories or artwork.

DC Comics, 2900 West Alameda Ave., Burbank, CA 91505
Printed by Transcontinental Interglobe, Beauceville, QC, Canada. 4/20/18. First Printing.
ISBN: 978-1-4012-7866-3

Library of Congress Cataloging-in-Publication Data is available.

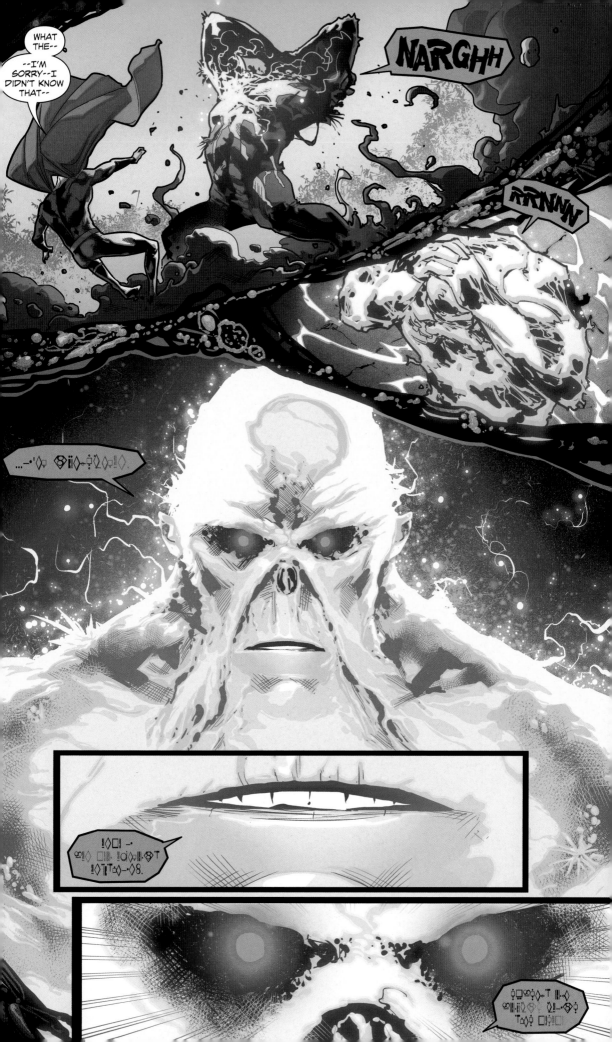

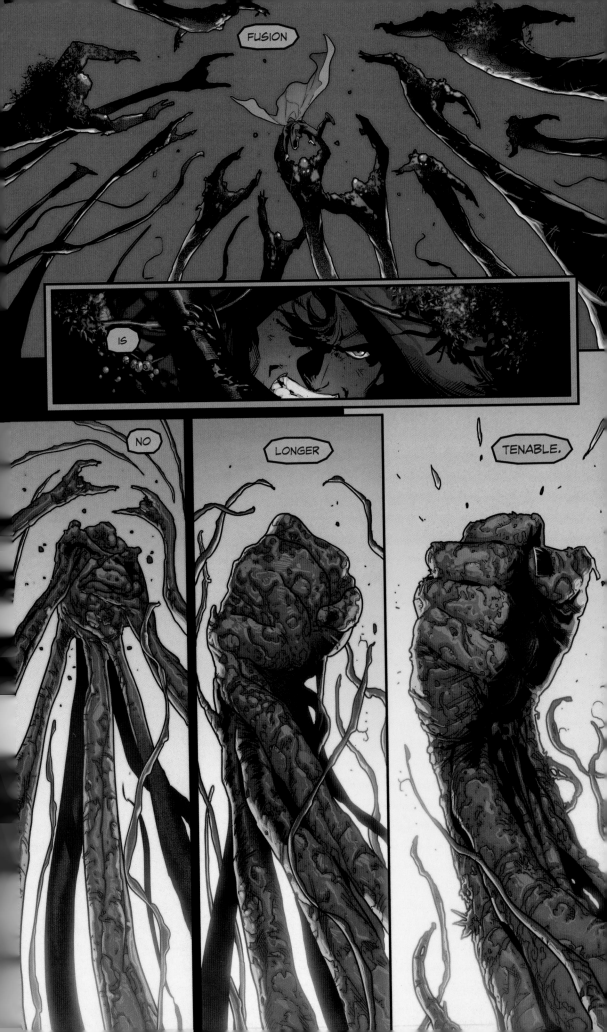

"...BUT IT MAY ALREADY BE TOO LATE!"

...LOOKS LIKE YOU WERE RIGHT, DAD...

...THE PICTURES *DON'T* DO IT JUSTICE...

...IT'S THE KINDA PLACE YOU *HAVE* TO LOOK AT WITH YOUR OWN EYES.

I WISH YOU COULD HERE TO SE WITH ME.

KENAN KONG.

YEAH, THAT'S ME.

YOU ARE ON THE LYST.

LIST? THESE GROTTOES WERE THE ONLY THING I WAS GOING TO HIT ON MY LIST TODAY...

BUT JUDGING BY TH LOOKS OF YOU, GRUESOME...

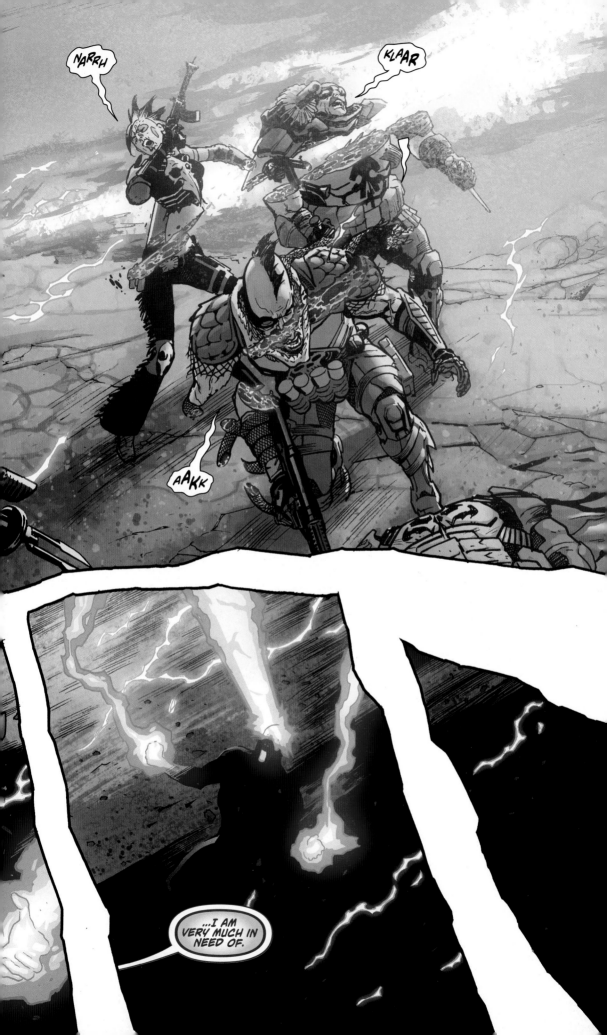

MULTIPLICITY

PART 2

PETER J. TOMA
PATRICK GLEAS
STO
RYAN SOO
ED BENES, CLAY MA
& JORGE JIMEN
ARTIS

...SO LET ME GET THIS STRAIGHT...

WE'RE STANDING IN A COSMIC POLICE PRECINCT THAT EXISTS IN A PLACE YOU CALL BLEEDSPACE THAT CONNECTS TO OTHER DIMENSIONS...

...AND RIGHT NOW, ALL OF YOU HERE ARE THE INTERDIMENSIONAL COPS WHO KEEP LAW AND ORDER BETWEEN ALL THESE EARTHS?

JK. DINEI RIBEIRO. ULISES ARREOLA

J ALEJANDRO SANCHEZ COLORISTS

JK COVER   ROB LEIGH LETTERER

JREW MARINO ASSISTANT EDITOR

JIE BERGANZA GROUP EDITOR

NO. WE DO **NOT** GET INVOLVED IN THE DAY-TO-DAY ASPECTS OF THE WORLDS THEMSELVES.

IT'S THE BIG PICTURE WE FOCUS ON-- **ONLY** THE OUTSIDE THREAT OR FORCE THAT ENDANGERS THE SECURITY AND STABILITY OF THE MULTIVERSE ITSELF.

A THREAT TO ONE EARTH IS A THREAT TO **ALL** EARTHS.

EACH OF THE EARTHS HAS ITS OWN PROTECTORS, ITS OWN LEAGUES.

AS I MENTIONED EARLIER, ALL OF US HERE ACTUALLY REPRESENT SEVERAL OF THOSE LEAGUES.

YOU ALSO MENTIONED THE SUPERMEN AND SUPERWOMEN OF THESE WORLDS ARE BEING TAKEN, WHICH BEGS THE QUESTION--

WHY WEREN'T **YOU** AND THE OTHER **SUPERS** OF YOUR EARTH ALSO ABDUCTED?

EXACTLY, AND WHY WAS ONLY **KONG KENAN**, THE NEW SUPER-MAN IN CHINA, ON THEIR LIST AND--

WARNING!

THERE'S A PART OF ME THAT WAS IN AWE OF MEETING SO MANY COUNTERPARTS. FROM THE START, I WAS ALONGSIDE A SUPERMAN WHO IS THE PRESIDENT OF HIS U.S. AND IT JUST GOT STRANGER FROM THERE.

VOICES AND FISTS RAISED IN ANGER ON SOME WORLDS...

...WE MADE OUR NEXT STOPS AS QUICKLY AS POSSIBLE.

...WHILE OTHERS WERE MORE INCLINED TO LISTEN TO REASON...

...AS WE THREW CONCEPTS AND SITUATIONS OF DIRE CONSEQUENCES AROUND HARD AND FAST.

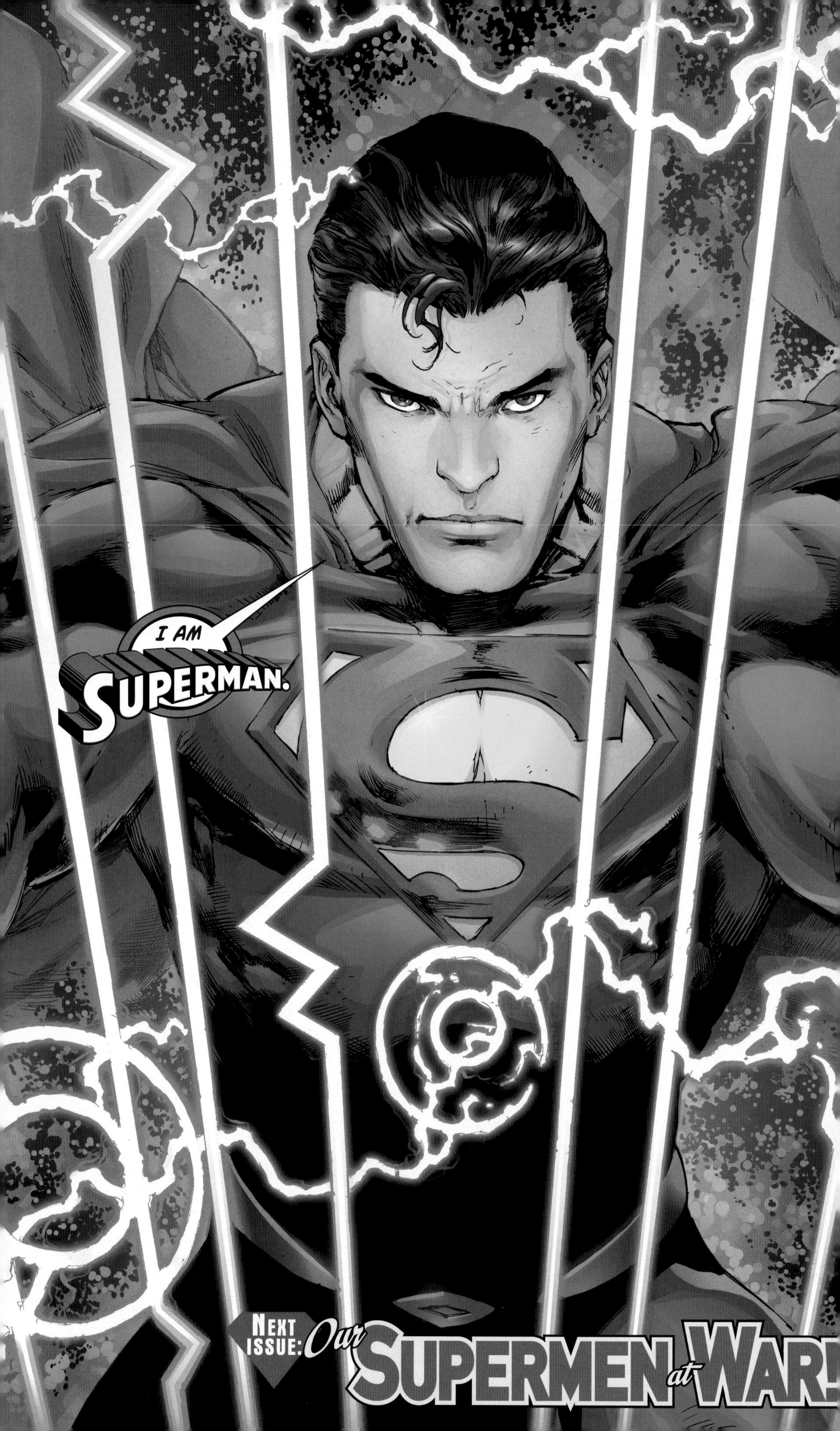
I AM SUPERMAN.
NEXT ISSUE: Our SUPERMEN at WAR!

A SUPERMAN YOU SAY, *hmm?*

YOU POSSESS THE POWER I NEED AND YOU MAY INDEED LOOK LIKE ONE...

...BUT ACCORDING TO MY DATA YOU ARE NOTHING BUT AN *ANOMALY...*

WHAT ABOUT ALL THE OTHER PLANETS FILLED WITH INNOCENTS?

SO, YOU'RE GOING TO BE THE *SAVIOR OF THE UNIVERSE, hmm?*

PETER J. TOMASI PATRICK GLEASON STORY

TONY S. DANIEL & CLAY MANN PENCILS

SANDU FLOREA & SETH MANN INKS

DINEI RIBEIRO COLORIST

ROB LEIGH LETTERER

IVAN REIS. OCLAIR ALBERT. MARCELO MAIOLO COVER

ANDREW MARINO ASSISTANT EDITOR

EDDIE BERGANZA GROUP EDITOR

MULTIPLICITY CONCLUSION

"WHAT ARE YOU ALL DOING BACK HERE?!"

NO "HAPPY TO SEE YOU ALIVE, AND THANKS FOR NOT MAKING ME THE SOLE SURVIVOR OF THE JUSTICE LEAGUE INCARNATE"?

OKAY, HAPPY TO SEE YOU ALIVE, AND THANKS FOR NOT MAKING ME THE SOLE SURVIVOR OF THE JUSTICE LEAGUE INCARNATE.

WHAT ARE YOU ALL DOING BACK HERE AND WHERE'S THE SUPERMAN FROM NEW EARTH?!?

THE SUPERMAN YOU REFER TO SAID HE'D ACT AS BAIT AND TOLD US NOT TO WAIT.

YOU LEFT HIM ALONE OUT THERE IN THE THULE-- IN THE MIDDLE OF NOWHERE-- WITH THIS PROPHECY FREAK EATING SUPERFOLKS FOR BREAKFAST WITHOUT A PLAN?!

HIS PLAN WAS US, RACER.

HE DIDN'T WANT TO LEAVE THE EARTHS UNPROTECTED UNTIL HE WAS SURE IT WOULD WORK.

ND WHAT PLAN WAS THAT?! OR HIM TO COMMIT SUICIDE HILE ALSO LOSING A ONE-OF-A-KIND VESSEL LIKE THE--

IT'S SOME KIND OF SIGNAL COMING FROM THE ULTIMA THULE... ...A LOCATOR BEACON.

...IT'S SINGING TO US.

THE SHIP... WHEREVER IT IS...

...DIDN'T THINK *THIS* WAS THE WAY OUR *FIRST* MEETING WOULD GO.

NEITHER DID I, BUT DON'T WORRY. EVERYTHING WILL WORK OUT FINE.

UNWARRANTED CONSUMPTION OF TIME.

DIG DEEPER.

ZZRAKK

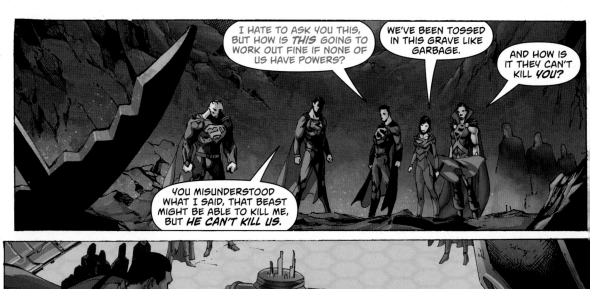

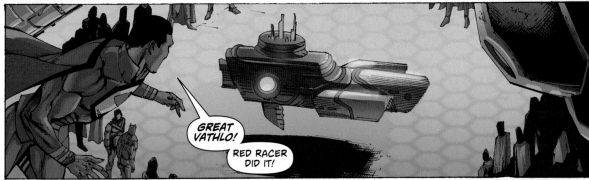

TAKE HIM DOWN HARD AND FAST, PEOPLE!

LET'S SHOW HIM WHAT A FEW SUPERFOLKS CAN DO!

THE MULTIVERSE DARES ATTACK ME!

WHAT IS HAPPENING--HOW IS ALL YOUR POWER RETURNING?!

POOM

POOM

WE'RE DONE BEING YOUR LAB RATS!

AND HAVING OUR POWERS STOLEN!

PAYBACK TIME!

LET'S JOIN THE FIGHT!

HIT PROPHECY FROM ALL SIDES.

NO MERCY UNTIL HE'S DOWN!

SHRRIPP

TOGETHER-- AS ONE UNIT-- TAKE OFF HIS HAND!

NOOOO!

I AM THE SAVIOR OF THE MULTIVERSE!

I AM ALL THAT STANDS BETWEEN US AND--

WHAT'S THAT ENERGY AURA AROUND HIM SUDDENLY?

THE LOWER HALF OF HIS BODY-- IT'S DISSIPATING--

--OBLIVION!

HE'S GONE-- SOME KIND OF TRANSPORTER FIELD.

WHERE DID HE GO?

HOPEFULLY WHERE HE CAN NO LONGER DO ANY HARM...

...AND HOPEFULLY WHATEVER PROPHECY WAS GETTING READY TO BATTLE WAS A FIGMENT OF HIS IMAGINATION OR VAIN-GLORY.

RED RACER DIED TO GET THAT OTHER THULE BUILT.

HIS LAST WISH WAS TO GET EVERYONE HOME, AND THAT'S EXACTLY WHAT I'M GOING TO DO...

"...OUR FIRST STOP IS NEW EARTH."

THIS IS THE LAST PLACE BESSIE WOULD GO TO...

BUT THE TRACK KEEP GOING...AN YOUR GRANDPA TELL YOU TO ST OUT OF HERE.

MY GRANDPA COULD BE HURT OR WORSE...

I HAVE TO GO.

YOU COMING?

Um, YEAH... I'M RIGHT BEHIND YOU.

I'M C-COLD, JON...

...CAN'T HOLD ON MUCH LONGER...

I HEAR SOMETHING...

MOOOO

OH NO-- IT'S BESSIE AGAIN! SHE FOUND US!

AND SHE'S GETTING READY TO DROWN US IN MILK!

WHAT ARE YOU CRAZY KIDS DOING DOWN THERE?!

YOU ALL RIGHT?

WE'RE OKAY...

ANY SIGN OF A FIFTY-FOOT SHADOW MAN?

NOT THAT I CAN SEE!

I'M BRINGING YOU UP!

KRRREEEK

I GOT YOU, KATH.

I KNOW, JON.

I'M JUST GLAD YOU KIDS DIDN'T GET HURT.

WE WERE WORRIED ABOUT YOU OUT THERE ALL BY--

BESSIE WAS IN AN AMBLIN' MOOD, WASN'T ABOUT TO LET HER GET LOST AND HURT.

I'M AN OLD COOT, DON'T GO WORRYING ABOUT ME.

THE STUFF WE SAW-- IT WAS SO CRAZY AND WEIRD--

IT'S THAT SWAMP. I TOLD KATHY NOT TO GO IN THERE--ESPECIALLY WHEN YOU DON'T KNOW YOUR WAY AROUND.

SOME OF THOSE BOGS EMIT GASES--BREATHE IT IN AND YOU CAN START *HALLUCINATING*--WARPED VISIONS AND ALL...

...WHICH, FROM WHAT YOU BOTH SAID, SEEMS TO BE EXACTLY WHAT YOU GOT HIT WITH.

I BETTER GET HOME BEFORE I WORRY MY MOM AND DAD.

SEE YA, KATHY.

GOOD NIGHT, JON.

SAY HELLO TO YOUR FOLKS, JONATHAN!

LATER, MR. COBB.

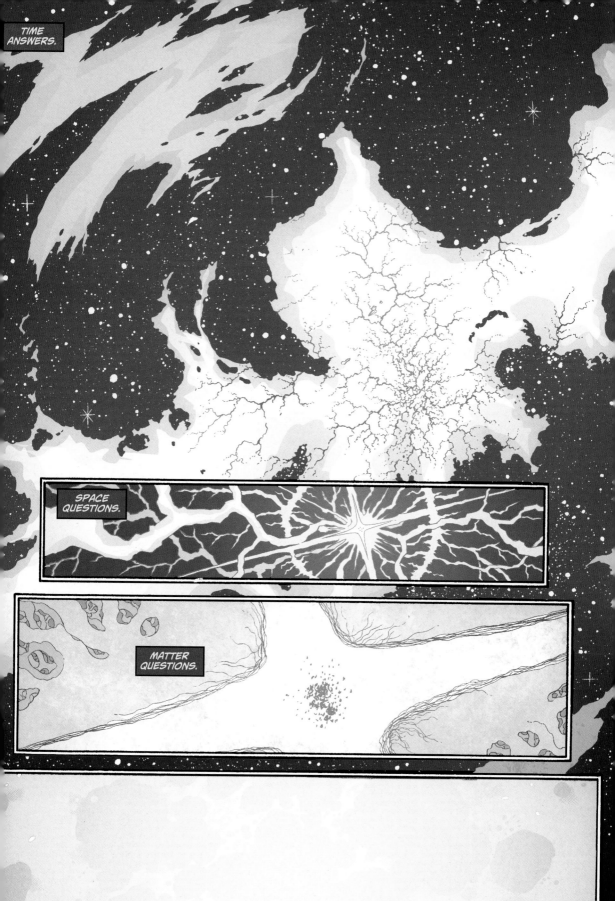

HOLLOW SPACES
WAITING TO BE FILLED...

...TO BE
WATCHED.

NO.

HAHAHA

HAHAHA!

HAHAHA!
YOU
COULDN'T
KEEP US
ALL!

SOMEONE
GOT *OUT!*

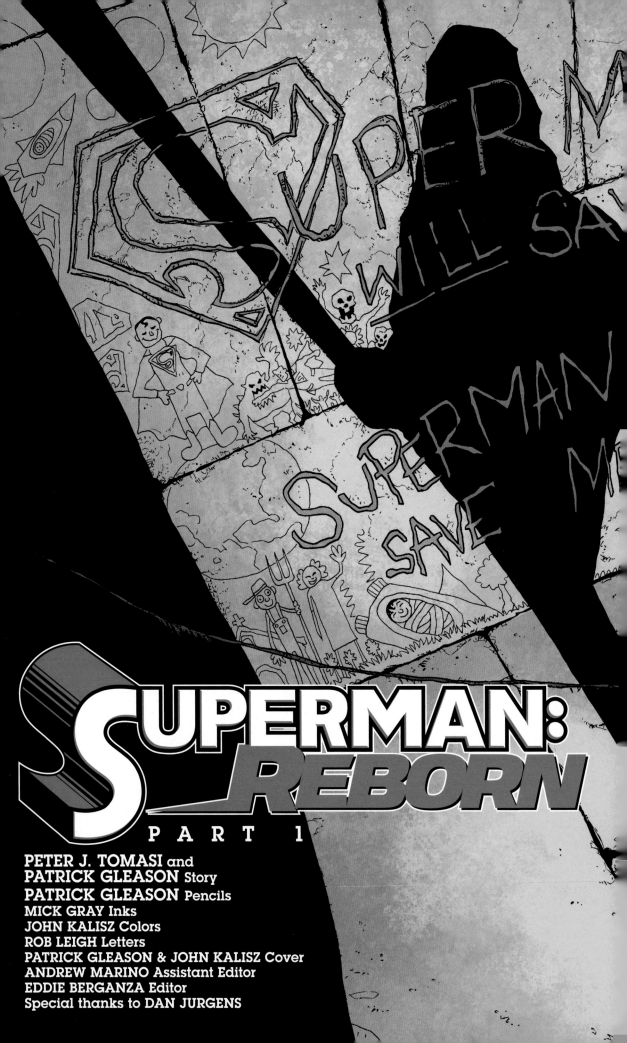

SUPERMAN: REBORN

PART 1

PETER J. TOMASI and
PATRICK GLEASON Story
PATRICK GLEASON Pencils
MICK GRAY Inks
JOHN KALISZ Colors
ROB LEIGH Letters
PATRICK GLEASON & JOHN KALISZ Cover
ANDREW MARINO Assistant Editor
EDDIE BERGANZA Editor
Special thanks to **DAN JURGENS**

SUPERMAN REBORN

PART 3: DON'T PASS GO

PETER J. TOMASI and PATRICK GLEASON Story
PATRICK GLEASON Pencils
MICK GRAY Inks ▪ JOHN KALISZ Colors ▪ ROB LEIGH Letters
PATRICK GLEASON & JOHN KALISZ Cover
ANDREW MARINO Assistant Editor ▪ EDDIE BERGANZA Editor
Special thanks to DAN JURGENS

For the full story, see SUPERMAN: REBOR

BLACK DAWN
CHAPTER 1

PATRICK GLEASON and **PETER J. TOMASI** Story
PATRICK GLEASON Pencils
MICK GRAY Inks • **JOHN KALISZ** Colors • **ROB LEIGH** Letters
PATRICK GLEASON & **JOHN KALISZ** Cover
ANDREW MARINO Assistant Editor
EDDIE BERGANZA Editor

JUST... BEAUTIFUL.

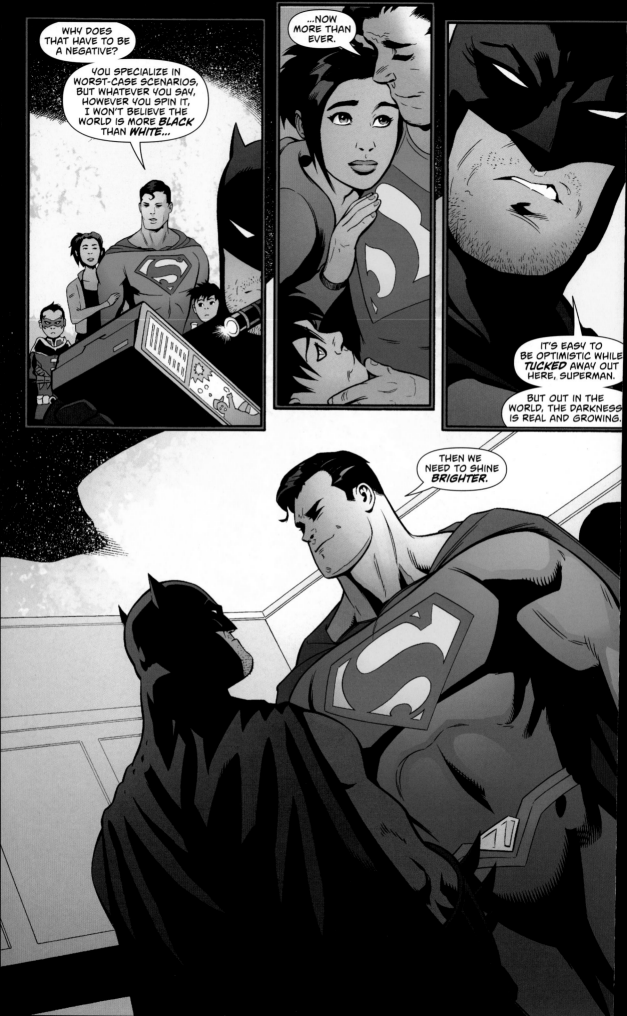

WHAT'S ALL THIS?

DID WE CATCH ANOTHER TROUBLEMAKER?

Hrrn...

DON'T WORRY YOURSELF, BESSIE. WE'LL PUT HIM WITH THE OTHERS.

HE WON'T HURT YOU ANYMORE. I PROMISE.

WHO...

...ARE...

❊

NEXT ISSUE: POWERLESS

BLACK DAWN
CHAPTER 2

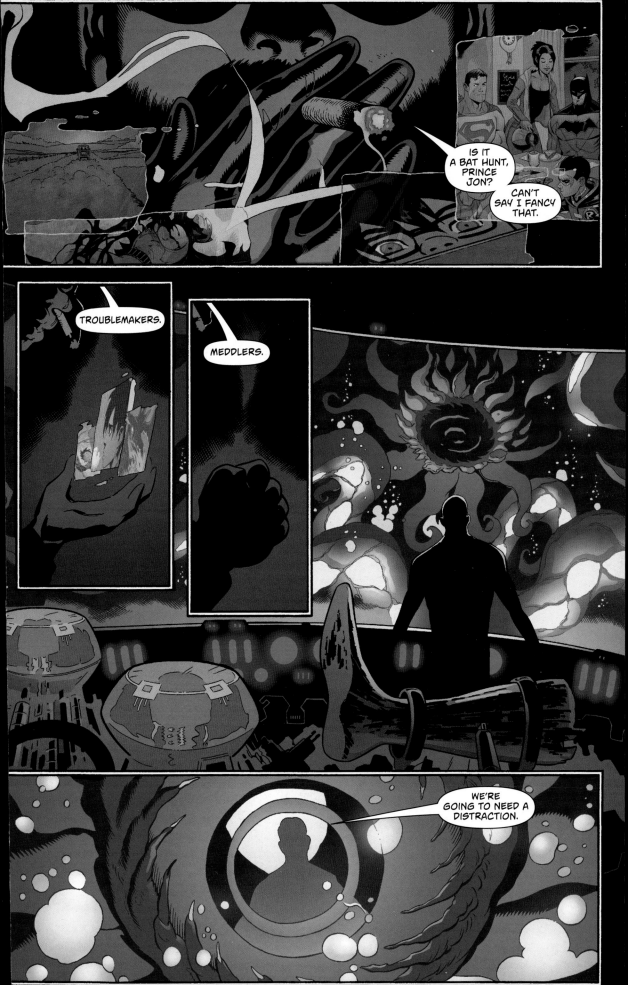

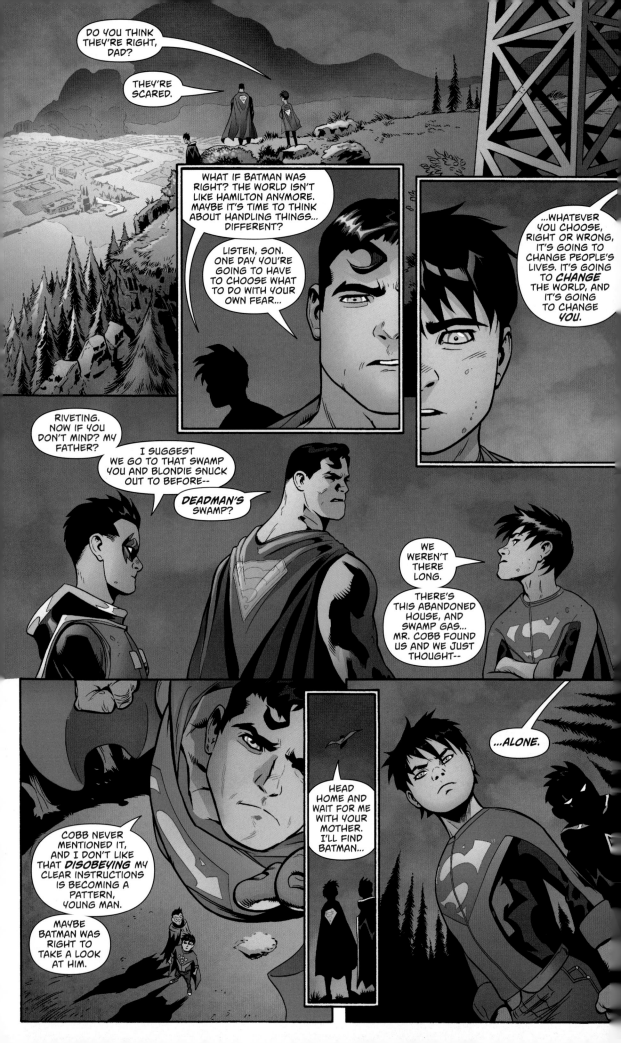

"...YOU'RE *SPECIAL*, JON."

"MORE THAN YOU KNOW.

"NO ONE WILL HURT YOU...

"...EVER.

"I PROMISE."

NEXT ISSUE: HANDS that ROCK the CRADLE

IT DOESN'T FEEL RIGHT JUST WAITING HERE.

I SHOULD BE OUT WITH THEM... LOOKING FOR BATMAN...

BZZT

BZZT

BZZT

BZZT

BZZT

IT HASN'T STOPPED.

IT'S BEEN ONE THING AFTER ANOTHER.

EVERY TIME WE EXPECT THINGS TO JUST GET A LITTLE BACK TO NORMAL...

...WE'RE RUDELY REMINDED THERE'S NO SUCH THING...

...BECAUSE EVERYWHERE WE TURN...

GOLDIE'S GRAVE...

JON!

CLARK!

'EVENING, MR. COBB. HI, KATHY.

SCRREECH

EVERYTHING OKAY THERE, MRS. KENT?

THE BIG OAK'S ON FIRE. DID YOU SEE ANYONE SET IT?

I HAVEN'T SEEN OR HEARD ANYTHING.

I WAS ABOUT TO HEAD OVER MYSELF AND INVESTIGATE. CALLED THE FIRE DEPARTMENT, TOO.

OH... JON AND I LOVED THAT TREE...

WHERE ARE YOUR BOYS? I HOPE THEY WEREN'T CAUGHT UP IN ALL THAT COMMOTION IN TOWN.

NO WORRIES, THEY'RE FINE.

ALL RIGHT, RUNDOWN ON WHAT WE KNOW: **BATMAN** AND **ROBIN** COME TO THE HOUSE, WORRIED ABOUT JON...

BATMAN GOES OUT BY HIMSELF TO DIG AROUND...

POOF. BATS DISAPPEARS.

THIS GIANT **SQUID** ATTACKS THE TOWN.

CLARK, JON AND DAMIAN TAKE IT DOWN.

THEN, NOT A WORD FROM THEM.

POOF, JUST LIKE BATMAN, THEY'RE GONE AND--

CANDICE?

THE PICTURES I SAW OF HER...

HOW'S SHE ALREADY UP AND ABOUT AFTER GETTING INJURED?

SHE'S HEADING FOR THE TOWN HALL...

Hmm, LOWER LEVEL...

WHY'S SHE TAKING THE BACK DOOR?

CREEEERK

DIDN'T REALIZE IT WENT DOWN THIS FAR...

ONE OF THE TOWN'S BOMB SHELTERS DURING THE COLD WAR.

ALL THE CIVIL DEFENSE SIGNS...

WHAT'S HAPPENING?!

THE WHOLE TOWN... A LIE...

CLARK!

JONATHAN!

ONLY ONE THING LEFT TO DO...

...HAVE TO USE IT NOW...

...THE JUSTICE LEAGUE EMERGENCY COMMUNICATOR BEFORE...

SHE'S A BIT MORE WELL-ARMED THAN WE ORIGINALLY THOUGHT.

WHUMP?

SKASSH

B-DEEP
B-DEEP

UPSTAIRS-- HURRY!

B-DEEP
B-DEEP

DOWN HERE!

SHE'S ALREADY OUTSIDE!

B-DEEP
B-DEEP

GET HERrRAAH!

VVRIAKZ

B-DEEP
B-DEEP

REQUEST AN IMMEDIATE COMMUNICATION LINK...

VROOOOM

...TO THE JUSTICE LEAGUE!

WHAT'S HAPPENING?!

KLAKK

PLIKK

UNIT BEING RENDERED IMMOBILE-- DISMANTLED BY--

TANGG

SNAPP

KRAK

POP

UNNFF

GAHH

HELLO, LOIS.

POWERLESS

POWERLESS

CHAPTER 4
BLACK DAWN

PETER J. TOMASI and **PATRICK GLEASON** Story • **DOUG MAHNKE** Pencils
JAIME MENDOZA, MAHNKE and **KEITH CHAMPAGNE** Inkers

WIL QUINTANA & **ROB LEIGH** **RYAN SOOK** **ANDREW MARINO** **EDDIE BERGANZA**
HI-FI Colorists **Letters** **Cover** **Assistant Editor** **Editor**

WHEN DID HAMILTON BECOME GROUND ZERO FOR MONSTER CENTRAL?

I CAN'T JUST SIT AROUND, CLARK--WE NEED TO FIND JON!

KLEEERK-K

IT TOOK OUT THE SUPPORT BEAMS!

RUN!

HOLD ON!

TAKE COVER, GENTLEMEN...

FROOMSH

IT HASN'T BEEN EASY FOR THE FIVE OF US TO HOLD BACK OUR TRUE POTENTIAL, BUT WE HAD TO FOR SUPERBOY'S SAKE.

HOSTILE INCOMING!

THIS IS YOUR LAST CHANCE TO STEP UP, BOY SCOUT. PROTECT THOSE YOU CARE ABOUT AND HELP US *KILL* THESE MONSTERS!

RAAIIKK

THOOM

RAAIKK

SUPER ELITE? JON?

MR. MARTINEZ, ISN'T IT? YOU'VE APPOINTED YOURSELVES AUTHORITY FIGURES AROUND MY SON TO DO *WHAT* EXACTLY?

TO *TEACH* HIM. SOMEDAY WE WILL NEED HIM TO SUCCEED WHERE YOU FAIL.

STAND DOWN. THIS CREATURE LIVES UNTIL I CAN GET TO THE *BOTTOM* OF THIS AND WHO'S IN CHARGE!

STAY OUT OF OUR WAY, SUPERMAN.

NO. WE CAN STILL TALK--

REEIIK

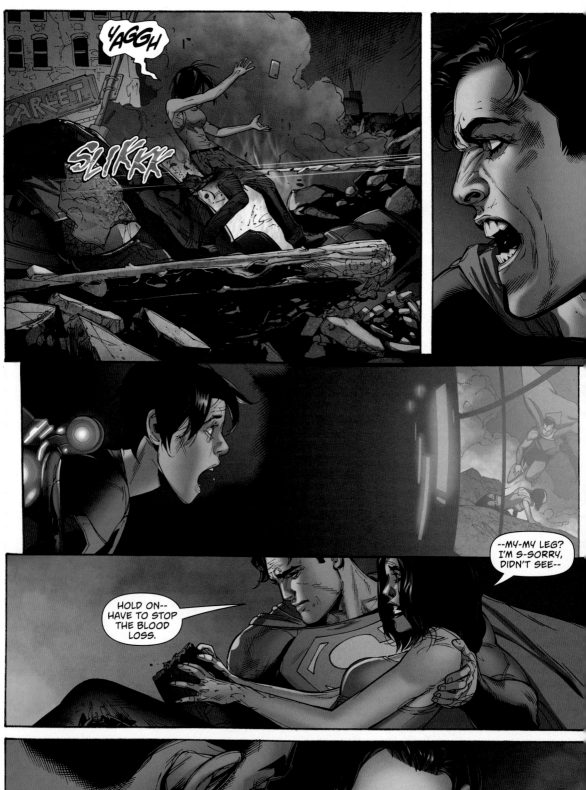

I'M AFRAID I CAN'T HAVE YOU TURN AWAY.

IT'S NECESSARY YOU WITNESS THIS.

ACTION EQUALS REACTION. THE TIME TO SWALLOW ANGER IS OVER.

WHY BE SORRY AFTER THE FACT...

...AND LET THE PAST BECOME OUR FATE?

DON'T WORRY, BABY. I'LL FIND HIM...

...JON... JONATHAN...

...BUT FIRST I'M GETTING YOU TO A HOSPITAL.

...AND MANCHESTER BLACK SAYS IT'S TIME WE HAVE A NEW SUPERMAN IN TOWN, MATE.
NEXT: INNOCENCE LOST

CHAPTER 5
BLACK DAWN

ATRICK GLEASON & PETER J. TOMASI Story • DOUG MAHNKE & PATRICK GLEASON Pencils
JAIME MENDOZA, MICK GRAY, JOE PRADO and DOUG MAHNKE Inkers

IL QUINTANA, JOHN KALISZ, HI-FI   ROB LEIGH   RYAN SOOK   ANDREW MARINO   EDDIE BERGANZA
lorists   Letterer   Cover   Assistant Editor   Editor

WE HAVE NOTHING LEFT! OUR PLANET IS **SCORCHED** IN WAR! MY GRANDDAUGHTER IS ALL I HAVE LEFT.

PLEASE, WE'LL DO ANYTHING TO NOT LIVE WITH THIS FEAR ANYMORE.

ALL IN FAVOR?

SKRSH

UFF--

THWAM

WE ALWAYS KNEW I'D FIND MY WAY BACK. CARRYING A TORCH FOR YOU, AND ALL THAT.

MY TREE... IT'S STILL BURNING?

CALL IT A TELEPATH'S VISUAL AID.

GAVE ME HEAD A WOBBLE AROUND SPACE-TIME FOR A WHILE.

FOUND MY WAY BACK TO SETTLE THE SCORE.

BUT LO AND BEHOLD THERE WAS A CHILD.

FWMMMMM

I SAYS TO MYSELF, CHESTER OLD MAN, THE DAD'S A DUD, WE ALL KNOW THAT, BUT THIS KID? HE HAS A CHANCE TO BE *GREAT!*

S-STOP IT, YOU'RE HURTING--

SHUSH, LAD. THE ADULTS ARE TALKING. NOW WHAT WERE WE SAYING?

S-SIC H-HIM!

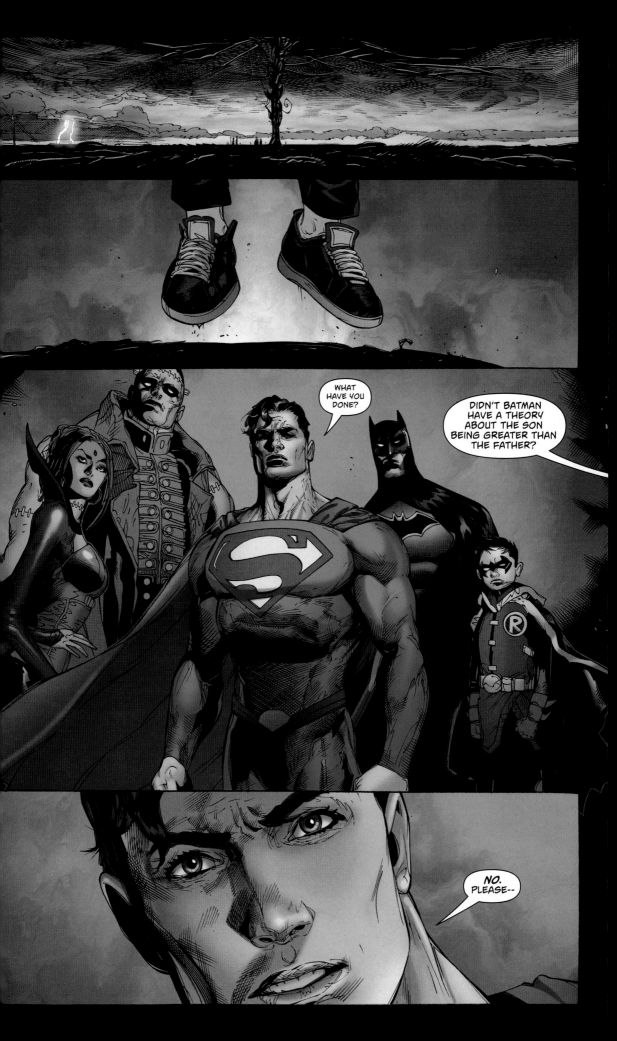

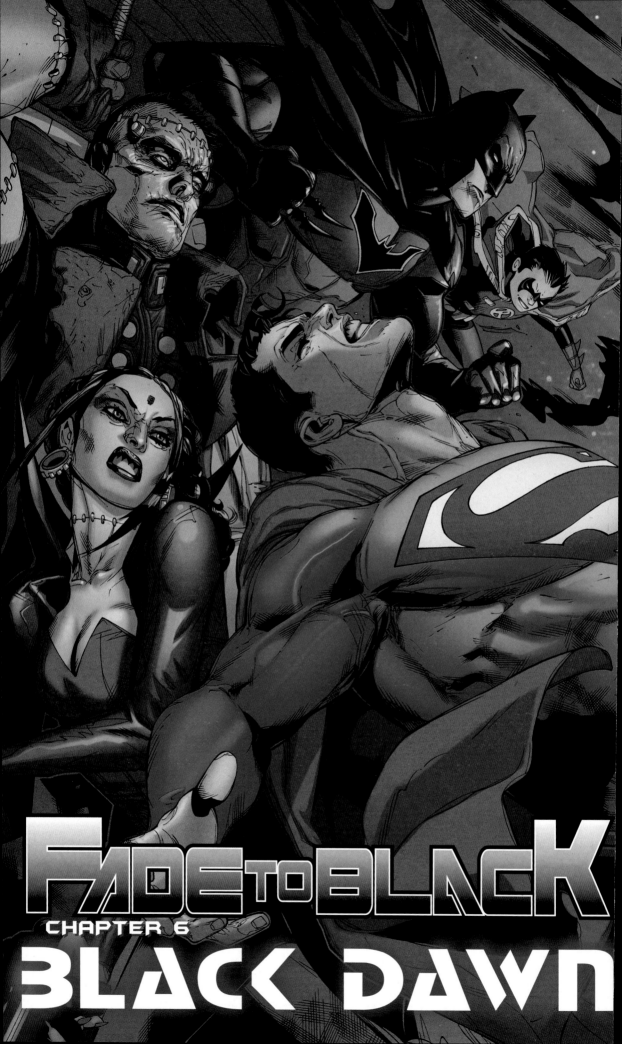

PATRICK GLEASON & PETER J. TOMASI Story • DOUG MAHNKE & PATRICK GLEASON Pencils
JAIME MENDOZA, MICK GRAY, JOE PRADO, RAY McCARTHY, SCOTT HANNA & MATT SANTORELLI Inkers
WIL QUINTANA & JOHN KALISZ   DAVE SHARPE   RYAN SOOK   ANDREW MARINO   EDDIE BERGANZA
Colorists   Letterer   Cover   Assistant Editor   Editor

TRYING TO SWEET-TALK OL' CHESTER?

WHAT ABOUT YOUR HUSBAND-- AH...

...CLEVER GIRL.

TZZRRKK

BUT YOU'RE NOT THE ONLY ONE WITH BACKUP, LUV.

MONSTER!

YOU WON'T BE THE FIRST CHILD I'VE DISPATCHED!

DON'T BE SO HARD ON THE LAD. HE'S NEW...

...CAN'T MAKE AN OMELET WITHOUT BREAKING A FEW EGGS, YA'KNOW?

FWASSSH

NO!

HUMPTY DUMPTY SAT ON A WALL...

HUMPTY DUMPTY HAD A GREAT FALL...

ACK!

PLK

SHLORRRRRP

FWUMPP

ALL THE KING'S HORSES, AND ALL THE KING'S MEN...ET CETERA, ET CETERA, MATE.

CLARK...

I KNOW...YOUR WORST FEARS COME TRUE.

NOW WITH BLACK, SUPERBOY COULD BE UNSTOPPABLE.

I SAW HIS BODY LANGUAGE *CHANGE* WHEN YOU TALKED TO HIM.

HIS HEART IS TRAPPED BUT IT'S STILL *LISTENING*. THAT BOND BETWEEN PARENT AND CHILD IS OUR ONLY HOPE RIGHT NOW.

ROBIN AND I WILL TAKE CARE OF THE FRANKENSTEINS AND THE REST OF THE ELITE...

I'LL DRAW JON AWAY FROM BLACK.

OL' MAN'S RUNNIN', M'LAD...

BRING ME BACK HIS CAPE. GOTTA USE THE LOO SOON.

NOW, SUPERBOY BLACK...

WOW. LOOK AT THEM GO.

HE'S GOING TO BE SAD TO LEAVE THESE WIDE OPEN SPACES.

HAMILTON WILL ALWAYS BE JON'S TOWN. LIKE SMALLVILLE IS MINE.

DO YOU THINK THEY'LL BE ALL RIGHT UP THERE? MAYBE I SHOULD--

RELAX, SMALLVILLE... HE COMES FROM GOOD STOCK.

HAVE I TOLD YOU HOW MUCH I LOVE YOU, MISS LANE?

TELL ME AGAIN.

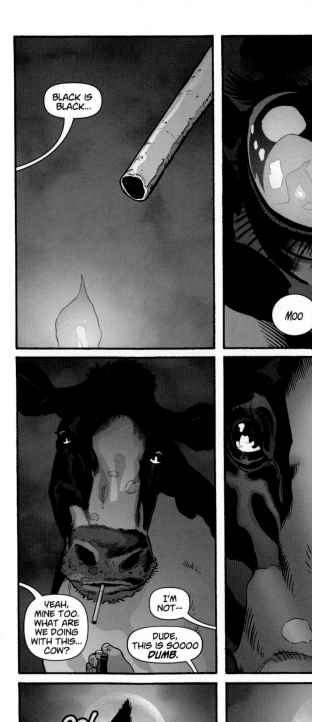
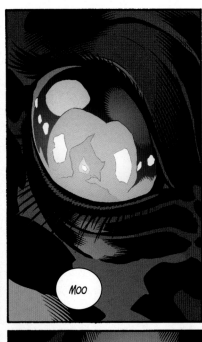

"YES, JON, YOU *DID* SAVE THE MOTHER AND DAUGHTER FROM THE BURNING BUILDING.

"BUT I WANT YOU TO *REALLY* ASSESS THE SITUATION NEXT TIME.

"THAT BEAM COULD'VE BEEN SUPPORTING THE ENTIRE CEILING, AND WHEN IT FELL...

CRRRRKK

"...IT COULD HAVE BROUGHT THE ENTIRE HOUSE DOWN ON ALL OF YOU.

"YOU JUST HAVE TO--"

I KNOW, DAD. I HAVE TO DO THINGS *YOUR* WAY. JUST LIKE HOW I SAVED THOSE TRAILERS FROM THE MUDSLIDE, OR THAT BANK ROBBERY I STOP--

THAT'S NOT WHAT I'M SAYING. YOU DON'T HAVE TO DO THINGS LIKE *ME*, YOU JUST HAVE TO MAKE SURE YOUR DECISIONS ARE THE *RIGHT* ONES.

THERE'S NO MARGIN FOR ERROR WITH WHAT WE DO.

TAKE T TRAIN

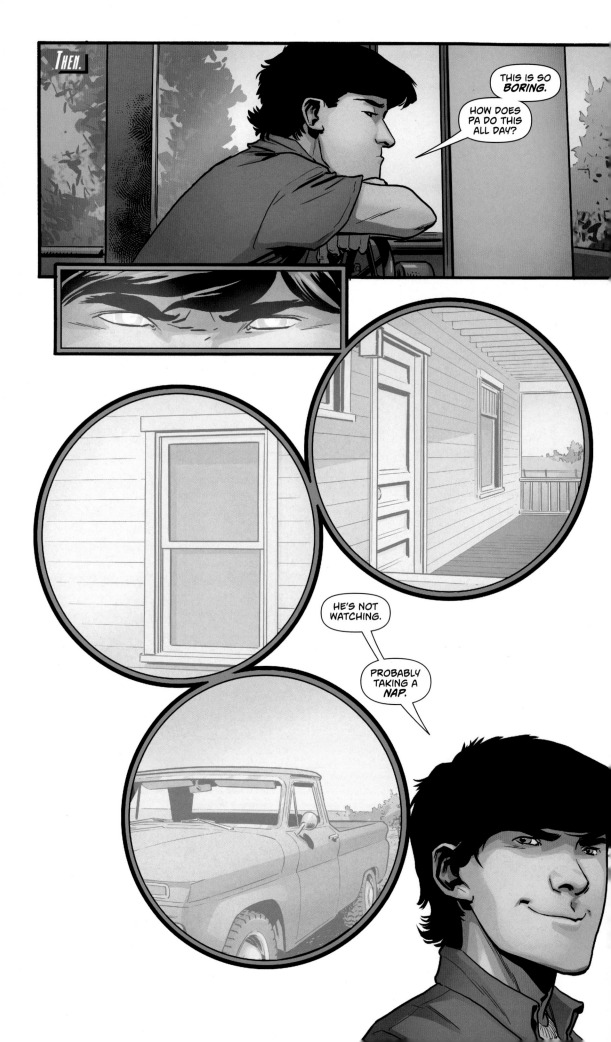

YOU MADE A MISTAKE, BUT SO DID I.

I SHOULDN'T HAVE EXPECTED YOU TO DO THINGS MY WAY-- WE'RE NOT THE *SAME* PERSON.

SO, YOU'RE NOT MAD?

I AM, BUT I'M JUST AS MAD AT ME AS I AM AT YOU.

I THINK WE BOTH NEED TO *APPRECIATE* WHO WE ARE AND HOW WE DO THINGS A LITTLE MORE. ESPECIALLY SINCE OUR SITUATION IS A LITTLE...

WEIRD?

LET'S CALL IT... *UNIQUE.*

NOW COME ON, MA HAS LUNCH READY.

WE DON'T WANT TO KEEP HER WAITING.

PA WAS PRETTY AWESOME, WASN'T HE?

HE WAS, AND I HAVE A LOT TO LEARN FROM HIM. BUT YOU KNOW WHAT?

WHAT?

THERE'S NO ONE ELSE IN THE WORLD I'D RATHER LEARN WITH.

Variant cover art for SUPERMAN #14 by Andrew Robinson

Variant cover art for SUPERMAN #15 by Andrew Robinson

Variant cover art for SUPERMAN #16
by Tony S. Daniel and Tomeu Morey

Variant cover art for SUPERMAN #19 by Gary Frank and Brad Anderson

Variant cover art for SUPERMAN #21
by Jorge Jimenez and Alejandro Sanchez

Variant cover art for SUPERMAN #23 by Jorge Jimenez and Alejandro Sanchez

Variant cover art for
SUPERMAN #24 by
Jorge Jimenez and
Alejandro Sanchez

Variant cover art for SUPERMAN #25 by Jorge Jimenez and Alejandro Sanchez

AFTER FRED RAY

SWAMPED

Script excerpts from **Peter J. Tomasi** and **Patrick Gleason** and preliminary art by **Jorge Jimenez** for SUPERMAN ANNUAL #1

PAGE 1

Dawn. Open the story with a close-up on some DEAD LETTUCE in the ground. The following panels should then show us that we're in Hamilton County, the Smith Farm, as CLARK, frustrated, stands there alone in blue jeans, with a loose blue jean jacket over a red work shirt, and work boots. He's not too happy at the moment as he reaches down and pulls a head of lettuce from the dirt and examines it then tosses it to the ground amid the other dead heads of lettuce. He thinks aloud: "Pa made it look so easy." He doesn't understand why the fields need so much water lately. "We've had plenty of rain, why are they so brittle?"

PAGES 2 and 3

Clark takes off in a blur from the field, and as he flies at super-speed, we'd like to have him change within the speed blur into his Supes uniform. Now in his Supes uniform, he scans the ground below and sees several ponds and streams and lakes he's familiar with in the vicinity have drained almost completely, revealing assorted junk and random garbage at the mucky bottom, which we'll see more closely in a moment.

Supes stares hard, using his x-ray vision, and he can see that below/beneath the lakes are various sinkholes, which have resulted in them draining.

PAGES 4 and 5

Double page spread, Jorge. I'd shoot it from behind Supes so we can get the real scope and feel as the most disconcerting thing he sees is just under the ground, leaving behind a trail of raised dirt in its wake. Supes spots TENDRILS OF ORGANIC MATTER–SWAMP THING'S tubular vines–snaking like worms from all directions off the pages, rippling toward an empty lake below him in the center of the page. Think of it, Jorge, like the creature from that movie *Tremors*, except it's not just one creature, but dozens of vines the size of fire hoses.

In the middle of the page is the raised FACE OF SWAMP THING, YELLING AT SUPERMAN from the now largely empty muddy lake below. To help visualize what we're thinking of, Google FACE ON MARS and that'll give you the feel we're aiming for.

SWAMPY: YOU DON'T BELONG HERE ANYMORE, SUPERMAN! (Please use distinctive Swamp Thing lettering and balloon.)

PAGES 8 and 9

These two pages will get across some info, Jorge, so whatever you can do to spice up the camera angles would be great.

Supes asks, what did Swampy mean, and Swampy tells Supes that being the environmental elemental knucklehead that Swampy is, and tied into the Earth in such a distinct way, that he was drawn here to Superman in particular. Swampy tells Supes that something is out of whack—a vibrational aberration that is tied into the way he draws solar energy from the sun that is different from the previous New 52 Supes.

Supes thinks about the aspects of some odd stuff that's come up recently—for example, in Geoff's REBIRTH, the scene at the hotel, and of course our first issue where he left the blue hand energy outline. No need to flash back, Jorge, we'll cover it in dialogue as Supes relates these recent problems and the death of the New 52 Superman to Swampy.

Remember, the situation is still tense, but Supes tries to convince Swampy that there's nothing to fear from him, he's here to help, here to do what the New 52 Superman did. As Supes speaks, he rests his hand in a friendly gesture on Swampy's shoulder...

PAGE 10

...which leaves behind a BLUE HANDPRINT OUTLINE on Swampy's body...

...and in turn causes Swampy to start suddenly turning all blue, as the energy handprint outline spreads like BLUE VEINS all across his head and body, infecting Swampy and causing his WHOLE BODY TO TURN BLUE (except his eyes, which should remain red)...

PAGES 11 through 13

...and putting Swampy into a trance-like state as he suddenly starts speaking Kryptonian (think of that scene in *The Lord of the Rings*, when Galadriel, played by Cate Blanchett, goes into that weird trance) while blue vines from his body start shooting into the ground all around Supes like straws, trying to draw/suck elemental power from the Earth/dirt to keep the blue at bay.

As this occurs, Supes steps back, looking at his normal hand in surprise, trying to calm Swampy down as Swampy suddenly snaps out of the trance and lashes out at Supes, his arms growing as thick as tree trunks as he swings at Supes and knocks him around a bit at the lake bottom. The whole time Supes continues to try and help, taking hold of the blue vines snaking off Swampy's body and trying to use them to wrap him tight, control him and calm him, but it doesn't work as...

PAGES 14 through 17

...we go for a ride!

PAGES 18 and 19

Cool shot as they explode out of the lake bed and Supes is knocked from Swampy as Swampy dives sideways under the ground.

Supes, all beat up, stands there waiting to see Swampy emerge, but instead, thick vines (no longer blue) shoot up from the ground and start wrapping around his legs and feet.

Supes uses his heat vision like a scalpel, trying not to burn Swamp Thing too much, as he attempts to cut away the vines, but it's too much and they really start getting a good grip on him, so let's have a lotta fun with Swampy's powers here as...

Supes takes to the sky, but the vines are still attached and trying to pull him back. He struggles as the vines wrapped around him start getting thicker and thicker, as do the ones from the ground. Think of it, Jorge, like Supes is trying to escape the clutches of the classic Beanstalk from Jack and the Beanstalk.

PAGES 20 through 27

We're doing comic books, right? So these next few pages should be insane, as we literally have Supes locked in a midair battle with Swampy as he fights the vines with his heat vision and also trades massive punches and whatever else you think could be cool, Jorge, as Swampy's body manifests itself in different vines and fights back as it tries to drag Supes down. In other words, think of, like, half a dozen of the vines looking like Swamp Things as the fight swirls around the clouds and some birds as they swoop in and even pull off food from Swampy to eat.

The sequence should end as Supes is really entangled by the vines that now turn into one big massive Swamp Thing hand (think of it like the size of King Kong's hand in the Peter Jackson movie) as it drops back to the ground where we once again see the FACE ON MARS SWAMP THING on the ground with its mouth wide open and the big Swampy hand FEEDING Supes directly into it!

The last image should be of Supes, entangled, wrapped tight, sinking into the black mud of Swamp Thing's mouth, the black mud like quicksand, pouring into Supes' open mouth as he slowly disappears under it until nothing remains but complete blackness.